IMAGES
of England

THE SODBURYS

The Boot Inn at Chipping Sodbury where Murray Dowding says that 'beer is sold by the pound'. The figure by the street light is Florence Jane Carter (later Williams) who was the daughter of Alfred James Carter, the landlord whose name adorns the pub sign and who died in 1916. The kneeling figure in front of the shed is 'Pongo' Ashton who sold second-hand goods. To the right of the Boot Inn there used to be a walled enclosure, which was the town's pound. It was here that straying animals were kept until the owners paid a fine to get them back. They were looked after by 'The Hayward of the Ridings' who was a steward responsible for the pound. If the owner did not come forward after a reasonable length of time, the animals were sold.

The new St Adeline's church in Little Sodbury, the building of which started in 1859, pictured around the time of the First World War. The wall to the village school is on the right and the land belonging to Church Farm on the left.

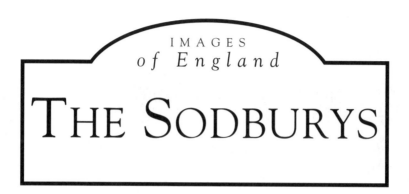

IMAGES
of England

THE SODBURYS

Compiled by
Yate District Oral History Project

TEMPUS

First published 1999
Reprinted 2000
Copyright © Yate District Oral History Project, 1999

Tempus Publishing Limited
The Mill, Brimscombe Port,
Stroud, Gloucestershire, GL5 2QG

ISBN 0 7524 1611 1

Typesetting and origination by
Tempus Publishing Limited
Printed in Great Britain by
Midway Clark Printing, Wiltshire

Cover photograph: Miss Holborow's private school, at Springrove in Old Sodbury, a beautiful house which stands back on the corner of Badminton Road and Common Mead Lane. Miss Holborow, who is standing on the left of the group of three on the garden path, gazes proudly upon her genteel charges at the turn of the twentieth century. The single-storey building on the left was specially built as a schoolroom, but has now been converted for Mrs Limbrick into a sun lounge. Here the Baptist Minister's children attended school and Dorothy Parker is second from the left, with her brother Robert, in the Eton collar, seated in front of her.

Contents

At the Chipping Sodbury Pageant are, standing, from left to right: William (Saddler) Allen, George Hillier, Arthur Clark, -?-, Leslie Williams, Bill Savory, Ron Swift, Gwyn Davies. Front row, kneeling: Tommy Dando, Clifford Powell.

Acknowledgements

The following people or organisations were kind enough to loan or donate material, give advice or assist in other ways during the preparation of this book:

Irene Benjamin, Tom Bennett, Sheila and John Bullock, Brenda and Richard Cary, Chipping Sodbury Cricket Club, Clerk to Little Sodbury Parish Meeting, Hubert Coleman, Barbara Cotterill, Suzanne Dando, George Davey, Sid Dunkerley, John Edgar, Jill Edwards, Derek Febry, Joan Febry, Marjorie and Tink Gibbins, Pete Greenaway, Margaret Hare, Vivian Harris, David Herbert, Maurice Horder, Joy and Bob Jordan, June and Tom Kent, John King, Allan Marshall, Fred Marshall, Dennis Matthews, Tony Matthews, Joy May, Lynda and Barry Miller, Gladys Nelson, Ray Pearce (author of *Potted History of the Perretts*), David Perrett, Jeremy Penfold, Peggy Porter, Ted Purbrick, Shirley Rogers, Dr Tony Sarafian and Jennifer Sarafian, Muriel Sherborne, Vera and Frank Shepherd, Phyllis Smith, Flo and Joyce Sullivan, Janet Sweatman, Eric Tily, Gordon Tily (author of The Three Sodburys), Margaret and Paul Tily, Peggy Trace, Joan and Norman Trotman, Martin Walker, Ann Ward, Tim Ward, David White, Kath Watkins, Paul Whittle, Tom Wigmore, Leslie Williams, Peter Williams, Robert Williams, Bernard and Kathleen Wooles, Revd Chris Wray, Annie Wright, Yate Heritage Centre.

Introduction

In producing this photographic and historical record it seemed a natural course of action to link together the three Sodburys – Chipping, Little and Old. They have a natural affinity, lying at the southern edge of the Cotswolds, with known settlements in the Little Sodbury area dating back to the Iron Age and records of later occupation by the Romans in the first century AD.

We must pay particular tribute to two local historians. Firstly, we owe a great debt of gratitude to Murray Dowding for his unique and extensive photographic work undertaken in the early years of this century and secondly to Percy Couzens for his detailed historical research over many decades until his death in 1992.

The Yate and District Oral History Project has had access to a wealth of information, mainly from private family photographs and individual postcard collections, which have been generously loaned by members of the three communities and interested people further afield. In addition, many anecdotal recollections have been provided which help to bring alive the visual images but with so much material available, it is also inevitable that a lot has been left out..

The photographs in the book depict street scenes and shops long since disappeared, country lanes and pursuits, sporting and leisure activities together with family portraits and colourful characters. While the costumes may have changed considerably, these portraits show that the joy and sadness, pride and resignation, loves and expectations revealed in the faces of our forebears were little different from our feelings today. Yet, in the face of great hardship arising from ill health, poverty and unemployment, they had a strength of community spirit and family unity, which transcended their sufferings and privations. The churches and chapels, the pubs and carnivals, the companionship in the quarry and hayfields brought a contentment that we seem to have lost today.

Yate and District Oral History Project is an historical society established in 1987 whose aim is to record the ever-changing faces of the local communities. This book is a further example of its work following the successful publication of *Yate* in the same series in 1998. While compiling this book we have made every effort to be accurate in the use the information gained from many sources. However, if errors are apparent we trust that you will bear with us.

Chipping Sodbury High Street in the 1930s.

Foreword

I have on my shelf *Diary of a Cotswold Parson*, by the Revd F.E. Witts, who lived in Upper Slaughter. On 8 April 1833 he travelled through the Sodbury Vale and wrote, 'Passing through the village of Sodbury, we came to the market town of Chipping Sodbury, an old, triste and deserted looking place. Here the aspect of the county is uninteresting, pastured by ragged horses, donkeys and geese, and bordered by mean looking cottages, half-dilapidated, and a general air of discomfort prevailed'.

I have to say that this has not been my impression of the Sodburys today, now thriving communities, full of life and therefore sought after as places to live. As a lover of history, I am grateful to the Yate District Oral History Project for finding the pictures and the anecdotes to enable us to fill in the past and to see how we have reached the present.

It is always good to review the past and it is pleasing that the communities have kept their character and some parts have even been improved. I suspect no-one for instance mourns the passing of certain industrial works in Chipping Sodbury.

Memories are about people who make the communities what they are, gathering together in different ways. In the communities, the churches remain important focal points and there are good relationships with the relevant civic bodies, which is as it should be. I have no doubt that the Revd Francis Witts would be pleasantly surprised by the modern Sodburys, retaining as you can see from this marvellous collection of photographs much of the best from the past but also being forward looking.

The Revd Chris Wray
Priest in Charge, Chipping Sodbury and Old Sodbury

An elegant young lady, Miss Betty Horne, poses for the camera with Tiny her dog in a De Dion Bouton car in 1911 outside Red Lodge. She later became the wife of Dr Haig Sarafian.

One
Chipping Sodbury

The origins of the town of Chipping Sodbury are unusual. It developed in early medieval times some two miles west of the settlement at Old Sodbury. It was built to a strict plan, with buildings along both sides of the street fronting long burgage plots to the rear. First recorded in the ninth century, the name Sodbury has changed somewhat over the centuries, while 'Chipping', the Saxon word for market, came later.

The visitor standing at the brow of the High Street obtains a wonderful view over the town to the distant hills above Old Sodbury. Its glorious gabled buildings, the War Memorial incorporating the ancient market cross, the Victorian horse trough, The George Inn and Tudor House are but a few examples of the many items of interest. The Baptist and Catholic churches date back to 1656 and 1838, respectively, whilst the Anglican church was first dedicated as a chapel in 1284.

The livestock market and railway station have gone with the passage of time, as have the saddlers, the blacksmiths, the wheelwrights and the clockmaker. Other aspects of the town are but a memory, the New Year's Eve supper for the bell ringers, the parish breakfast following the Communion Service, the billeting of the North Lancs Fusiliers in the First World War, the gas street lamps and the dedication of the Cross in 1920 followed by tea for the children at Penglaze's cinema.

One remaining old custom is the Mop Fair. In 1932 it was reinstated in Broad Street after irregular openings for some years in the 'Rag Field'. Although many small traders have disappeared, quarrying and transport still provide a considerable amount of employment. Whilst modern developments have come at a certain cost, the vivid memories of horse-drawn vehicles of the independent traders, the personalities and events from a bygone age all help to compensate for much of what has been lost.

Rounceval Street at the top of The Bowling Hill, c. 1910. Stone slabs provided access across the gutter to the cottages. Notice the pump.

Rounceval Street, c. 1900. There appears to be some gossiping outside the lamp shop on the corner of Brook Street. The ivy covered house is now Dando's car showrooms and further along can be seen the Grapes Hotel.

The Old Vicarage once stood at the bottom of the Bowling Hill on the left-hand side where the MEB and South Gloucestershire Council Offices currently stand. The vicarage was an imposing three-storey building, having twenty-seven rooms and surrounded by three acres of garden. When a new and smaller vicarage was built in Horseshoe Lane Major and Mrs Cleaver took up residence in the old vicarage. Later came Mr and Mrs Ford who turned it into a vegetarian guesthouse and hired out the tennis courts for one shilling and six pence per hour. In 1940 the vicarage was bought by the MEB for £8,000 and was demolished in 1960.

Rock House, now a nursing home, was at the bottom of The Bowling Hill on the corner of Quarry Road. It is said that there are subterranean passages under Chipping Sodbury with two entrances on the west side of the town, one behind here at Rock House. There were connecting passages behind Hill House on the Parade and the Grapes Hotel in Rounceval Street. Early in the 1900s it was occupied by Mr Albert Vizzard who owned an aerated water and lemonade business which used marble stoppers in the bottles. Later he began a haulage business which operated from the back of the house.

The Elms on the right-hand side going down Culverhill Road, in the snow in 1963. How clearly this lovely house can be seen before the road was widened and Mr Reg Pullin had the high wall built around the property. The Elm trees are silhouetted against the sky, but now a housing estate has taken over, with Leaman Close on the left.

A view taken between the wars of Brook Street, leading down to Brook Road, and now roughly the site of Mill Lane, where quarry horses waded through the stream to keep the wheels of the carts damp and prevent shrinkage. The building in the centre was used as a cart shed, with a hayloft to provide for the horses. The cottage on the far right was the home of the carter, Mr Hodder.

The High Street, showing many different types of architecture, mainly from the seventeenth century. In Georgian times many of the gables were taken down and new facades added, covering the older stone walls. Behind these buildings long narrow burgage plots were laid out towards the River Frome.

In this view of the High Street in 1907 can be seen the Foxwell Memorial on the right hand side where it was originally erected outside the Reading Room. It was moved to its present position just inside the Baptist church gate during the Second World War since, it was said, the American servicemen found difficulty in avoiding it! Andrew James Foxwell was a stalwart of the Baptist church from the time he joined in 1874 until his death in 1903. It was his vision that led to the purchase and conversion of the New Schoolrooms in 1885/86.

There is not a person in sight in this view of the High Street, c. 1900. View House, now 'Moda', faces down the street and Tyndale House is on the far right, with bay windows. This was the house where the Revd Lemon's daughter ran a preparatory school in buildings out at the back. It has changed use over the years; it was once Tanner's Betting Shop and is now an Estate Agents.

The Clock Tower commemorating Lt Colonel George Blathwayt of Dyrham Park (1797–1871). He fought at Waterloo and the tower was built in his memory some ten years after his death. An unusual feature of the clock is that it has to be wound from the outside. The present toilet block was erected in 1948.

Chipping Sodbury Police Station c. 1910, or earlier, in the centre of the picture. It was built in 1862 on the site of the Duke William Inn to a design to be found in many parts of the country. The Petty Sessional Court, the lower building to the right, was added in 1878. Formerly the court had been held at the Cross Hands farm, now the Cross Hands Hotel, Old Sodbury. The last court was held in Chipping Sodbury in 1981, when a new court was opened in Yate, built on land forming part of the former Thorns Farm. On the left of the police station is the Old Grammar School.

The High Street, 1900. The pony waits patiently outside the Bell Inn, one of the three inns in the town to provide accommodation. Notice the ornate gas lamp over the bar window. Gas lamps were introduced into the street after the Chipping Sodbury Gas and Coke Company was formed in 1871. Previously the lighting was from oil lamps, and then only in winter time.

Hounds Road flooded in 1958/59. Ted Purbrick is on the left outside his shop while Adrian and Melody Purbrick paddle in the water. Daisy Pratley's cottage is first on the right. Daisy was a well known character who took it upon herself to boil fish to feed the cat population of the town! Further down the road are two cottages, built in 1735, which together had a mortgage of eight pounds in 1858 and were sold for twenty two pounds in that same year. These premises, now converted, are where Mr White the dental surgeon now practises.

The row of houses at the end of the Wickwar Road, formerly called Church Lane, which were demolished in the early 1960s to make way for road widening. The house on the corner is Bill Allen's Saddlery and next to it is a store shed used by 'Saddler' Allen and John Russell, the grocer who traded where Worthingtons is now located. Next is the house where the Nibblett family lived; Walt the father and his son were killed in the Second World War and their names are on the War Memorial. The last two houses in the row were occupied by Mrs Horlock and her family and Mr Tony Williams and his wife Joan, respectively. Further up the road was a fodder store owned by John Russell and a shed where hurdles, rails etc were stored for use on market day.

The George Hotel is the oldest hostelry in Chipping Sodbury. As early as 1439 pilgrims stayed here, perhaps on their way to Kingswood Abbey near Wotton-under-Edge. During the nineteenth century it was one of the three inns providing accommodation, the other two being The Bell and The Portcullis.

The Town hall, 1900s, which in the fifteenth century was a guild hall, for a Guild or Fraternity, not to be confused with a trade guild. One such trade guild in Chipping Sodbury was probably a guild of cloth weavers who used the chapel in St John's church as their guild hall. On the left of the town hall was the priest's house where two priests lived who also took the role of schoolmasters in the town. In 1549, after Henry VIII dissolved the monasteries, the town hall was sold and became a private dwelling again and the priests were no longer required to carry out their duties. It was only a short time before the burgesses bought the building and it became the town hall. It took on a new frontage in 1858 and at present it contains the town's mace and seal which was given by Ann, the Countess of Warwick, in the mid fifteenth century.

Tudor House in Hatter's Lane is probably the oldest house in Chipping Sodbury dating from c. 1480. The overhanging upper storey window was useful for throwing out waste into the road below while avoiding passing pedestrians – 'Gardez l'eau!' In the early 1900s it became a lodging house giving meagre food and shelter to those who did not want to go to the workhouse or Spike in Yate.

The River Frome flooding Hatter's Lane in 1910. The bridge probably had a ford next to it but both have now been replaced by a new bridge.

More flooding of the River Frome, in the early 1950s, going back towards the Church from Hatters Lane. Things still look pretty grim!

The Swan Inn, pre-1913, on the corner of Broad Street and Hatters Lane before it became Powell's cycle shop. To the left is the post office behind the telegraph pole and then what is now the NatWest Bank. Over the front was written 'The Old Bank House' before recent renovation.

The deep snow of 1963 in Horse Street. The tractor is parked outside Mr Harold Gough's shoe and drapery store. Mr Gough previously owned a shoe shop in Rounceval Street where shoes were made to order. The bus comes round the War Memorial to pick up passengers waiting at the corner of Broad Street and Hatters Lane.

Horse Street where, during the fifteenth and sixteenth centuries, there was a bar gate across the road, near to where the cyclist is standing, which prevented cattle wandering into the town. The house on the right with the pillars is Melbourne House, thought to have been the site of The White Horse Inn.

Horse Street in 1900. This part was known as The Green when Cross Keys, the third house on the left in the corner, was built in 1690 for a brewer called Leon Martin and his wife Isabel. It was sold to a yeoman, P. Reed, for £110 in 1708, sold again in 1720 to Mr Rogers, a merchant, for £100 and then another price decrease came when it was sold to Betty Trotman in 1771 for £84! She bequeathed the house to her maidservant Anne in 1793. Other professionals and traders have lived at Cross Keys, such as Samuel Richards, an apothecary, Robert Coates, a clergyman and Thomas Curtis Leman, a surgeon.

Station Road, now Badminton Road, in the early 1900s with Red Lodge and the Victorian Villas beyond. The horse and cart are coming from Chipping Sodbury and heading towards Smarts Green. Red Lodge was built for Mr Bertram Horne, father of Mrs Betty Sarafian.

A tranquil scene in 1912 in Badminton Road leading to the station on the right and Blanchards Farm on the left. One shaft of the Badminton rail tunnel can be seen on the skyline.

Looking north over Chipping Sodbury in the late 1940s. Horseshoe Lane, once the main route into the town from the south, passes Cotswold Road that has yet to become part of the by-pass. Chipping Sodbury School, built in 1939, is in the foreground and Barnhill Quarry to the north of town is still relatively shallow. None of the recent housing developments in this area have started to appear. To the right of the church is the Rag Quarry pool. This quarry had been deepened and had encountered a spring that was piped to provide a water supply to Brook Street. When the pipe was broken it was not repaired and the quarry was allowed to flood, becoming an unofficial swimming pool. In the 1920s it was also used as an ice rink in the winter. After several people were drowned it was declared too dangerous and it was filled in around 1950.

St John the Baptist church at the turn of the century looking over the rooftops of the cottages next to the Wickwar Road. This road was originally just an access road to the church with no bridge across the River Frome. Changes came in 1774 when the route was upgraded to become the main road to the north of the town; until then the main route to the north had been along Brook Street.

St John's church in the early 1900s from the northeast. In 1130 the 'Sopeberie' estate was owned by William Crassus who saw that he could increase his wealth by building a new town two miles west of Old Sodbury, far enough away from his own manor house. The first charter was obtained in 1220. The existing parish church at Old Sodbury, also called St John the Baptist, was too long a walk for the townsfolk of Chipping Sodbury wishing to worship, especially in winter. In 1283 a chapel of ease was built on the site where the church is today and it has been altered and extended over the centuries to produce the building that we know.

The church underwent a programme of restoration in 1869 under the guidance of the architect Mr G.F. Street. A three-tier pulpit was removed only to reveal a beautiful fifteenth-century stone pulpit.

As part of the restoration work a new porch was added into which was put this lovely statue of the Virgin and Child.

St John the Baptist church bell ringers in 1934 in the church tower, photographed by Murray Dowding whilst experimenting with flash photography. Back row, left to right: John Bethell, Gerry Townsend, Reg Freegard (captain), Wilson Hillier. Front row: Leslie Williams, Sydney Hobbs (church warden), Glen Hillier, Ivor Davey, Ted Townsend.

On New Year's Eve in the years preceding the Second World War, before ringing in the New Year, a dinner for the bell ringers was provided by Mr Hobbs the church warden. It was put on by Mrs Dagger at the Royal Oak and was much appreciated by all. The bell ringers fitted leather muffles to the bell clappers for ringing on New Year's Eve and they were removed once the New Year had arrived.

St Lawrence's Roman Catholic church near The Squire in Broad Street. Sarah Lunn who married the Revd Egerton Neve, the vicar of Old Sodbury, became on the death of her sister a very wealthy lady. She became a Catholic and in the 1830s bought the biggest inn in the High Street known as The Swan. It was a late-Elizabethan house with outbuildings. The main building became the presbytery and the large outbuilding at the back was made into a chapel known as St Lawrence's. In 1838 the Revd Thomas Rolling, of the Order of St Benedict, became the first parish priest.

St Lawrence's Catholic Church, Chipping Sodbury.

The Baptist chapel, Hounds Road, built in 1819 on the site where there had been a Baptist meeting house. There have been Baptists in the town since the 1650s who would have originally met in private houses and not in public until the Toleration Act of 1689. Painter's Mead is on the left, now a primary school.

Electric headlights and sidelights were a notable feature on this 1926 Clayton six-wheeled, end steam tipping wagon. It also boasted the amenity of cab doors, though there was of course no windscreen. Speed was restricted to 12mph, which was probably just as well with those smooth rubber covered solid tyres, which often would have been running on shiny cobbled roads. Forward visibility would have been abysmal too, with an enormous blind spot ahead of the vehicle.

The early days of the haulage business, *c.* 1920. Nine of the Febry family are shown with their mother and father. Standing along the front, left to right: Fred, Mr and Mrs A. Febry, Clara and Bill. On the bonnet Peggy sits on the left and Jean on the right. Sitting in the back of the truck, left to right: Frank, Bert, Bessie and Jo.

Dick Febry took his first and only driving lesson in 1921; it lasted ten minutes and was given by Mr Frank Bees who was the licensee of the George Hotel in Chipping Sodbury. He bought his first lorry, a First World War Peerless chain drive, on hire purchase for £650. He worked twenty-two hours a day to pay off his debt in six months. By 1930 he had bought a second lorry, a new Studebaker, and employed Mr Alfie Boucher and Mr Bert Seymour as drivers. When the Second World War broke out, in 1939, he had eighteen Leyland lorries. Dick Febry is seen here in the 1920s at Barnhill Quarry when he was driving a solid tyred lorry for a Gloucestershire haulage contractor.

The postwar period saw a great expansion to Dick Febry's business despite nationalisation in 1948. In the 1960s this one million-pound transport business was the biggest in the south west of England, employing 200 people. The Sodbury Queen Motor Coach Company formed part of these operations. Mr Febry is seen here on the left with his new Rolls Royce. Next to him are Maurice Ladd and Mr Ablett, both from Shellmex.

A charabanc outing in Chipping Sodbury, arranged by Mr Peachey, the tailor, for his family and employees 1930. Immediately behind the side screen, lerft to right: -?-, Alice Hawkins, Mrs Peachey, Mrs Peachey's sister, Reg Perrett, Mr Peachey, John Peachey. At the back: Kate Player, Nora Padfield, Hilda Dando, -?-, -?-, -?-, Kate Trotman, Mr Peachey's father-in-law, Percy (Poshy) Marshall, Owen Roberts, Gilbert Wheeler, -?-.

A Britannia Class loco at the station pulling the Red Dragon Express in the 1950s. It used to come through here at around 11:00am each day.

Chipping Sodbury GWR station before it was closed in April 1961. The milk train passed through at 7:15am, stopping at every small station along the line to Swindon to pick up milk churns and drop off newspapers. The sidings were busy unloading coal and loading up stone from the quarry.

Soldiers from the 5th Battalion Loyal North LancashireRegiment, commanded by Colonel Hesketh, by the clock tower opposite the Jack Russell Gallery which was once The Bell Public House. They can also be seen below outside the Grapes Hotel in Rounceval Street after coming up The Bowling Hill.

During the First World War army camps were established alongside the Wickwar Road, near to the church. The tracks through the camp and the perimeter of some of the tents have been marked out with stones. Around these tents, lettering seems to have been laid out in the borders. The pond is probably the Rag Quarry unofficial swimming pool.

Being so close to the town, soldiers were frequently to be seen in the main streets. The Mechanical Transport corps 494 A.S.C. appear to be undertaking some sort of work with their first aid lorry by the town hall. One of the most important events was payday which in this case appears to be near Christmas time with the Christmas tree in front of the tent. Perhaps Christmas started early that year since the card is dated 5th November 1915!

Outside the town hall during the First World War are the bandsmen of the Mechanical Transport Service Corps with Lieutenants Hampson and Thomas sitting at either end of the front row. The band then led the soldiers up to the common for drill.

Passing the town hall on 2 November 1916 is the gun carriage carrying the draped coffin of Sgt W.W. Wynnes. He was buried with full military honours.

Chipping Sodbury Red Cross workers in the First World War making splints, encouraged by the Dowager Duchess of Beaufort. The splints were possibly ready to use on the injured servicemen at Little Sodbury Manor or Horton Hall.

Queen Mary meeting the land girls during the Second World War. The Queen often visited local organisations whilst she lived with her niece, the Duchess of Beaufort, in Badminton House. Also in the picture is Mrs Connie Clarke, England's youngest land girl, standing on Queen Mary's right in a woollen sweater. She came to Court Farm, Codrington, from New Malden in Surrey. Later she moved to Raysfield Farm, at the bottom of Love Lane, which was owned by Miss Bushfield who was the organiser of the Land Girls in the area. When Raysfield Farm was sold to Hedley Newman of Thorn's Farm, Yate, she worked in both places until the Land Army was disbanded in 1952.

After the First World War cities, towns and villages erected monuments to honour those who had fallen during the hostilities. Chipping Sodbury erected its memorial at the end of Broad Street. Here the memorial is being dedicated on 31 March 1920. The buildings to be seen around the war memorial are from left to right: The Bank House (Jack Comely lived here) Powell's cycle shop, The School House (although the head teacher John Penglaze did not live here) the sweet shop on the corner (Mr and Mrs Dando) and lastly Mr Holberrow's house (clerk to the parish council).

On the war memorial can clearly be seen the sixteenth-century market cross which used to be at the end of Broad Street, but since 1862 had been stored for safe keeping in the Presbytery Yard. The cross, originally erected in 1553, was a sign to traders that all transactions were made in the sight of God and served as warning to them to be honest. To the right is an Elizabethan house that eventually became Mrs Thompson's sweet shop.

36

Cattle in Horse Street with their drovers in the 1920s. A weighbridge was situated outside the Town hall where the cattle were weighed and given a number. When their time came to be sold they were taken to the pens erected in Hounds Road, once called Chapel Lane. From there they were easily transferred to the auction ring which was outside the Old Grammar School, now the library. After the market was over some of the cattle would be driven all the way to the abattoir in Old Market, Bristol.

Market day in the 1920s. In 1954 the markets, held on the pitchings in the main street, came to an end when it proved impossible to comply with the new regulations which called for a second weighbridge and a covered selling yard. For as long as people can remember markets had been held on alternate Tuesdays in the town. Pens could be erected on both sides of Broad Street, one side of the first part of Horse Street and up to the Clock Tower in the High Street. Sheep pens stretched from Porter Stores (now the Beaufort Hunt) to the corner of Horse Street, calves were sold near the National Provincial Bank (now NatWest) and pigs were penned near the George Hotel. Horses were sometimes for sale but were held by their owners in the middle of the street. During the Second World War and afterwards animals were sold directly from the pens.

Parking has always been a problem, just like this Market Day 1920. On this day, the market must have been smaller since no pens have been erected up to the clock tower. Notice the First World War German field gun to the left of the clock tower. Upon request, these were distributed to various towns as war memorabilia after the Armistice. It was a favourite pastime for the boys of the town to 'fire' and climb all over the gun. The gun eventually disintegrated and ended its days on the Ridings.

The concrete plant of John Arnold and Sons in1928, by the Chipping Sodbury quarries, where they appear to be making not only concrete, but also prefabricated units and blocks. Note the gasholder by the gasworks in the background, which was sited in what is now Bennett's Court.

Hard graft for these workmen and their carthorses who are filling in the mill stream as part of the works to construct a sewer, 1928. The gentleman in the centre foreground is most probably George Hood who, despite having only one hand, spent all of his working life in the quarry. Life was less arduous for the onlookers, the children sitting on the wall. The house on the far right in Brook Street was that of the coalman, Bill Short, father of the well-known Minnie Short.

Barnhill Quarry in 1947 showing the dram-lines and drams which were used to haul the blasted stone to the storage bins and crushing plant. Stone was taken out of the quarry by road for both local distribution and to Chipping Sodbury station for use further afield. The quarry was started in the early 1800s and is called 'The Ridings' on the OS map of 1920. The present name is said to have come from the barn on the top of an adjacent hill. There were five quarry businesses operating at the turn of the century, including John Arnold and Sons who bought Barnhill in about 1876 and started quarrying. Barnhill Quarry closed in 1972, leaving a hole in excess of 0.8 miles long, but work continues in the adjacent Southfields Quarry, which was started in 1963. A tunnel under the Wickwar Road also gives access to Hampstead Quarry which was started in 1978.

Hauling stone from Barnhill Quarry to Chipping Sodbury railway station early this century. The steam engine is passing Mr Allan's saddlery, now demolished, at the bottom of the Wickwar Road.

On the corner of Broad Street and Hatters Lane in the early part of the twentieth century was Powell's cycle shop which had previously been the Swan Inn. The Swan had earlier transferred its licence to this site when the existing premises had been sold for conversion into St Lawence's Roman Catholic church. Mr Powell sold and repaired bicycles and also hired them out for 6d an hour!

A dreary wet day in the High Street for the bathchair and barrel organ, but the carnival proceeded nevertheless on 19 July 1919. From the left can be seen Sweatman's bakery, next the home of Mr Heddon (schoolmaster) and then John Hatherell's hardware shop before he moved further down the street. Adjoining are the premises of Mr Nichols, a paraffin dealer, later to become the location of Peachey's tailoring business. To the far right are the premises that at one time had been Vizard's brewery, but were converted in the early 1930s by Ernest Tily for John Hatherell's business.

Gale's grocery and drapery store on the extreme left, 1920s. It was later demolished and the site can now be seen as the archway leading to the NatWest car park. It was from Gale's store that grammar school uniforms were purchased.

Mr Fred Peachey, the bespoke tailor, with his dog Rupert outside his shop in the middle of the High Street 1930. Jones the ironmongers next door was previously Dunkerley's garage and is now Hatherell's. Mr Peachey's clothes were renowned countrywide and seemingly never wore out. His customers included private individuals and families, for example the Listers of Dursley, the hunting fraternity, jockeys, officers in the services and hospital consultants, to name but a few. He employed fourteen, and sometimes up to twenty, personnel under the general foreman Percy (Poshy) Marshall, who sadly died aged forty one. Mr Peachey's only son, John, emigrated to Canada after the Second World War.

The bakery in the High Street in the 1930s. Sweatman's bakery, with its double fronted shop and awnings, sold delicious home made bread and cakes. The horses and delivery carts went through the double doors, to the left of the shop front, and into stabling behind. On Sundays and at Christmas time joints of meat could be taken by the townsfolk to Sweatmans to be cooked in the bread ovens. Note the Foxwell memorial mentioned earlier.

Sweatman's bakery cart on Kingrove Common with the delivery lad Les Williams and Dolly the horse in 1934. Les was fifteen years old at the time and earned 7s 6d a week. He later trained as a bricklayer but a serious accident at the Portishead power station site resulted in a move back to Chipping Sodbury. Here he became a well-known figure as the local postman.

Prince plods slowly up the High Street between the wars hauling a load of coal, driven by Minnie Short who could hump a bag of coal as well as any man. Prince always refused to move on up the street unless he first received a carrot from Borrett's the greengrocers.

Horse Street, Chipping Sodbury.

Pullin's shop at No. 7 Horse Street in the 1930s with Mr Pullin's car parked outside. The shop sold a wide range of products including groceries, haberdashery and clothes. In fact Mrs Pullin would order anything, if it was requested. The store was later sold to Mr and Mrs Gough who sold clothes and haberdashery on one side and had a shoe department on the other. The latter was supervised by Miss Russell, who was Mrs Gough's sister.

Arthur Henry Skuse came to Chipping Sodbury in 1930 after working in a barber's shop next to Lane's the bakers in Yate; Charlie Greenaway negotiated the business deal. Here Mr Skuse, another well known character in the town with his 'short back and sides and eyebrows' and still working aged seventy three, stands under the barber's pole between Jack Sandells, the sports outfitters, and the International Stores.

Miss Annie Trotman (later Mrs Thompson) of Smarts Green Farm measuring milk from the churn for Mrs Murray Dowding on her delivery round 1936.

The Saddlers shop in the 1950s before the Wickwar Road was widened and the shop demolished. This shop was like an 'Aladdins Cave' for the boys of the town, selling Meccano, Dinky Toys and sports equipment. It was here that the leather footballs were repaired after weekend matches, taken in on Mondays and collected on Fridays, if they could be found! The scene is a quiet lunchtime, all the shops are closed and Dorothy Flook waits by the water pump for her friend Joan Febry to cycle along from Old Sodbury. They must be back at the quarry offices by 2 o'clock. Albert Greenaway cannot wait any longer and has turned right and headed up the Wickwar Road on his bicycle.

Murray Dowding. It is with immense gratitude to Murray Dowding (1881–1966) that the Sodburys and district have a photographic history of buildings, events, personalities and landscapes of the area. From the turn of the century he could be seen travelling on his bicycle, his equipment in his basket, attending functions or arriving at private houses to take family groups or single portraits. After the First World War he acquired a Douglas motorbike and sidecar to make life a little easier. He left a wealth of material for later generations to ponder on and admire.

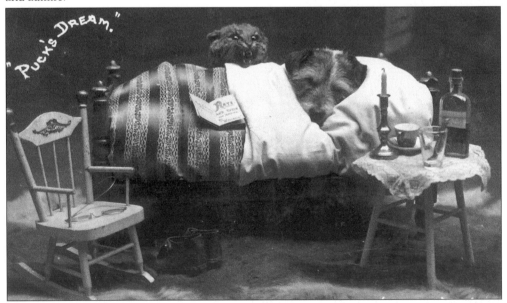

'Puck's Dream' shows Murray Dowding's beloved terrier Puck who accompanied his master everywhere and must have been the most photographed dog in the district. If one looks carefully he can be found in many of Murray's photographs.

Murray Dowding, his wife Gladys and his sons Marcus on the left and Ridley on the right. Murray Dowding continued trading in the ironmonger's shop in Broad Street, Chipping Sodbury after the death of his parents Marcus and Elizabeth. It was at the back of these premises in a converted wash-house that Murray processed his photographic plates. He was always quick with his repartee and often quite caustic to his customers. Woe betide anyone whom he saw entering a rival establishment in the street who later returned to his shop!

A typically superb study by Murray Dowding of the three Dunkerley brothers in the mid 1920s. On the left is Bob, in the centre Sid and on the right is Harold. Nellie the spaniel takes centre stage.

Walter Dunkerley driving a 1903 Vulcan. Before he set up business in his own right he was chauffeur and mechanic to the Duke of Beaufort, whom he often took to racing stables in Ireland.

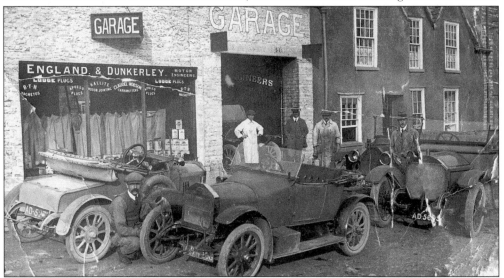

Walter Dunkerley joined Mr England as partner of this garage in the 1920s, which is now the premises of Hatherell's. A fine engineer, Walter Dunkerley began his career making oil engines in Southport, then travelled the country for the Vulcan Motor Company and later worked at the Renault factory in London after service in the Royal Flying Corps. He settled in Chipping Sodbury after meeting his wife in Malmesbury. The car on the far right is a Napier converted from a First World War ambulance to a touring car. It was the job of his son Sid to polish the brass radiator! Standing in the white overalls in the centre is Walter Dunkerley, with Reg Cole on the far right who owned a garage in Acton Turville.

Sid Dunkerley outside his premises in Broad Street, acquired by his father in 1930 from Mr John Penglaze. He attended Chipping Sodbury Grammar School, Bristol University and ultimately became a Member of the Institution of Mechanical Engineers. He was commissioned into the RAF in the Second World War and served in the Far East. On demobilisation he worked for both Napiers and Listers before joining his father's business.

Sitting on 'Black Bess' is Allan Grace with his friend Betty Horne, *c.* 1906. A cousin of the famous cricketer W.G. Grace, he later became a doctor and held surgeries on Sundays to enable him to hunt on Mondays. He took forceps with him to unlatch difficult gates in the hunting field.

The dolls collection. Opposite Allan Marshall's barber's shop, in the second cottage at the junction of Broad Street and Hatters Lane, lived Miss Daisy Florence Grace. She had a wonderful collection of dolls and here she is showing them to Bill Pullin, sitting on his father's car with his sisters, from the left Joy and Hetty, and Di Sweatman. Miss Grace was a cousin of the famous W.G. Grace.

Mr Herbert Perrett and his family 1910 at Hartley House in the High Street, that is currently occupied by Darlows the estate agents. Back row, left to right: Clifford, Elsie, Reginald. Middle row: Irene, Mr Herbert Perrett, Mrs Emily Perrett (née Rogers) Dorothy. Front row: Leslie, Nina, Leonard.

A delightful study for the Peace Carnival in July 1919, outside what is now Artingstall's butcher's shop in the High Street. We see the Tily family, from left to right: Bert, Eric, Roy, Rosa, Stan and Les. They are all in fancy dress except Stan, who seems to have entered the class for the best decorated bicycle.

During the First World War Belgian and American soldiers, as well as our own troops, were billeted in the town. Two rifles have been borrowed for this photograph by Dorothy Pullin on the left and Jean Sweatman on the right. Harry Dando, who stands in the middle, owned a garage business in Rounceval Street, currently Dando's Garage. He later sold it to Ivor Ball and then traded in a large china shop in Broad Street.

At Red Lodge, in Horse Street, waiting patiently on their horses in the 1920s are, from the left: Martyn Codrington (daughter of the veterinary surgeon and sister of Vera Thomas of Home Farm, Old Sodbury) Ivor Ball (founder of Chipping Sodbury Motors) and Betty Horne (daughter of the county surveyor).

Mr Bertram Horne on 'Firescreen' in the 1930s. Originally from Wootton Bassett, he became county surveyor and was involved with the railway line construction, including the building of the Badminton Tunnel.

A sunny June day in 1934 for the wedding of Eric Tily and Kit Griffin, photographed in the garden of 'Roscrea'. Standing, left to right: Ernest Tily, Janice Tily, Eric and Kit, James Griffin, Leslie Tily. Seated: Rosa Tily, Mollie Horn, Ida Green.

Family and friends at the wedding of Leslie Tily and Eileen Freeman on 17 December 1936, outside 'Roscrea' in the High Street. Seated, left to right: Ernest Tily, Janie Tily, Rhoda Freeman, Daphne Freeman, Norman Harris. Standing: Eric Barnard, Peggy Freeman, Leslie and Eileen, Stanley Tily, Frances Rice (fiancée of Eric Barnard). Sadly, Eric Barnard, a pilot in the RAF, was killed in action in the Second World War.

A group of some of the eighty men at one time employed in the building firm of Ernest Tily, pictured behind 'Roscrea' 1930s. From evidence gathered by Percy Couzens it would appear that the Tily family's forebears have probably been living in the Sodbury area since the early Middle Ages. From left to right: Fred Whitworth, Charlie Adams, Maurice Every, Stan Pinnegar, Jack Hardwicke, Arthur Hawkins, Tom Tuck, Tom Stokes, Walt Batten, Reg Woodman, Harry Wiltshire, Ted Vizzard, Frank Tanner, Mervyn Malpas, Fred Oakhill (foreman) Harry West (foreman) Harry Turner, Ernest Tily.

The dedication of the Standard of the Badminton Women's Section of the Royal British Legion in the late 1940s at Badminton church. Irene Tudor is carrying the Gloucestershire County Standard and bearing the Chipping Sodbury Standard is Mrs Thompson, wife of the well known local postman Harry Thompson. Immediately behind her is Mrs Beatrice Lewis carrying the Old Sodbury Standard.

The presentation to Mr and Mrs Lambert of a tea set, as a leaving present to mark Mr Lambert's position as the Chipping Sodbury postmaster in the 1940s. The presentation was made by Mr Jim Williams, the postman who lived in the Reading Rooms in the town. Front row, left to right: Bill Lewis, Jim Williams, Bessie Bristow (the postlady who delivered to Yate and Yate Rocks during the Second World War) Mr Lambert, Mrs Lambert, Harry Lewis. Back row: Tim Coleman, Harry Locke, Clara Seymour, -?-, Harry Thompson (father of Tony Thompson whose business was T.T. Motors in Hatters Lane).

Frederick Short with his horse and cart 1950. Fred Short lived in 'The Barton' behind 'Tudor House' and was a well known local character. He used his horse and cart to collect rubbish off the streets of Chipping Sodbury, before the council became responsible. He dumped the rubbish to the left of the common gate going towards Horton. He was always to be seen with his horse at carnivals and shows, where he was only too proud to display his horse brasses.

Allan Marshall, a well-known character in the town, began his career as an apprentice barber to Mr Skuse, whose establishment was near to the International Stores, (later changed to Worthingtons). Allan now has his own business at the bottom of Broad Street at the junction with Hatters Lane, and has been cutting hair for fifty years. He is known for his wit, his knowledge of local history and his collection of photographs and other memorabilia. He contributed many items for the production of this book. In this photograph work has stopped at Skuse's salon and Allan rests, hand on broom, with Penelope Borrett on the left and Diana Borrett on the right. These ladies worked in their family greengrocer's shop, which was in the High Street next to Artingstall's butcher's shop.

Dr Haig Sarafian, centre front row, with the Bristol City and Marine Ambulance Corps, Yate Division, photographed in the garden of 'Moda', his home and surgery in July 1936. Although born in Armenia he named his house after a suburb of Istanbul. It was in Turkey that he tended British prisoners in the First World War. He developed a great rapport with them and decided to come to England where he took a place at the Middlesex Hospital. He subsequently came to Chipping Sodbury to assist Dr Allan Grace, later taking over the practice and becoming a respected and much-loved member of the medical profession.

Major L. Montague Harris, a larger than life personality, who wielded tremendous influence in the town from his arrival in 1919 until his death in 1961. A native of Leicestershire, he attended Loughborough Grammar School and became a solicitor after war service, taking a partnership in Latchams and Montague. Some of his many interests and positions included Clerk to Sodbury and Lawfords Gate Magistrates' Court, Superintendent Registrar, Clerk to all the Sodbury Trusts and President of the Cricket Club.

Mr Percy Couzens, a local historian, was born in Old Sodbury in 1905. He first attended Chipping Sodbury Church of England school, when Mr Penglaze was headmaster, and then went to the grammar school. After leaving school he worked for the Great Western Railway, retiring in 1963. His great love was local history and we are indebted to him for his research and knowledge about the Sodburys which we still draw on today.

The Squire 1960, 'Time gentlemen please!' The last orders for the landlord and his wife, Mr and Mrs F. Collard on their retirement. This was prior to the arrival of Frank (Fatty) Febry as landlord. From left to right: Peter Hodkinson, Jack Rogers, Mrs Collard, Allan Marshall (hairdresser), Mr Collard, Albert Harman (taxi driver).

Miss Neil's private school, accommodated in what is now Lloyds Bank, was one of several private schools thriving in the town. In this picture of 1907 Miss Neil is seated with her pupils, boys and girls of all ages. Dolly Dando, later Mrs Reg Pullin, is standing sixth from the left in the back row.

The Baptist minister the Revd Aquila Lemon and his wife had a school for young ladies at Cotswold House in Horseshoe Lane at the turn of the century. When the Revd Lemon left the Manse, 1917, his daughter continued the school in the High Street in the building that is now occupied by the estate agents MacKendrick Norcott.

In the eighteenth century the Grammar School occupied the upper storey of The Garrett, which was one of several large buildings in Broad Street opposite the Royal Oak. In 1789/90 The Garrett was pulled down and the school was moved to the site of the ruins of the Lamb Inn. Today the building houses the library. The inscription, 'Old Grammar School' can still be seen carved over the door.

Chipping Sodbury Grammar School photograph, June 1916, taken in the Grammar School field, near the site of St John's Church of England school.

Giving out the prizes at the Grammar School's sports day, held on the field in 1923.

The Grammar School girls' hockey team, 1920. Standing, left to right: Miss Morley, Myrtle Lewis, Pixie Bond, Miss Richards (or Miss Booth?), Mr Waters (headmaster), Gladys Archer, Mary Morgan, Jessie ?. Seated: -?-, Pearl Waters (daughter of the headmaster), Winnie Raggatt, Phyllis Simmonds, -?-. The goalkeeper in the front is Rosa Tily.

The staff at Chipping Sodbury Secondary Modern school in 1953. The school had been situated in the Old Grammar School premises with extra temporary accommodation added behind. In 1939 a new grammar school was built in Cotswold Road and the pupils were transferred from the old school. Back row, from left to right:- ?-, Mrs Madison, -?-, Mr Willmott, Mrs S. Neilson, Mrs Harris. Middle row: Mr Bosanko, Miss Handle, Mr Sheen, -?-, Mr Gay, Miss Burcombe, Mr E. Evans. Front row: Mrs Champion, Mr Hart, Miss Watkins, Mr Pickles (headteacher), Mr Hayes, Mrs Hare, Mr Young.

The Secondary Modern school football team 1959. Back row, left to right: Mr Hayes, Martin Walker, Kenny Webber, George Shire, Chris Garland, David Orchard, Mr Naylor. Middle row: David Jardine, Pete Greenaway, Terry Witchard, Roy Bridgeman, Mike Thomas. Front row: John Febry, Benny Cresswell, Gordon Dando, George Hedge.

St John's Church of England school, in 1914, now Sodbury Masonic Hall, in Hatters Lane with Mr Penglaze the headmaster and his wife standing at each end of the back row. Percy Couzens, later to become the well-known local historian, is sitting at the left end of the front row.

A family school photograph taken by Murray Dowding in 1921 at the back of the St John's Church of England school. Back, left to right: Harold Williams (twelve years old) Edith Williams – later Edith Coleman (fifteen) Alfred Williams (fourteen) and, on the chair, Leslie Williams (about four). Teachers at the school were Mrs Bazely, Miss Simms, Mrs Witcombe, Mrs Penglaze and her husband John Penglaze the headmaster.

The Church of England school concert, 1922/23. Back row, left to right: Tom Tily, -?-, Jim Clements (later a window cleaner), Frank Jones, Agnes Williams, Nora Clements (later Mrs Frank Rogers), Stella Gowen, -?-, -?-, -?-. Front row: Sid Dunkerley (garage owner), Eileen Bodman, Claud Digby, Les Williams (later a postman) Dick Trotman, M. Lumber, Les Davey, Janet Styles, Joan Matthews, Gwen Clark.

A smartly dressed woodwork class at St John's Church of England school, c. 1937. The photograph was taken on a Tuesday afternoon after a morning spent gardening further down Hatters Lane, by the side of the River Frome. After much practice with mortice and tenon joints under 'Boss' Knight, they turned their skills to teapot stands, trinket boxes and scrapers for their gardening tools, to mention just a few of the objects produced. Back, left to right: Ted Watkins, Wilf Norton, Stan Hill, Bob Dunkerley, Roy Trotman, Ray Mills. Front row: Clifford Moulder, Ray Pearce, Roy Curtis, Ted Watts, Fred Marshall.

The Horse Parade of 1906, one of the annual parades of heavy draught horses. What a sight it was to see, with the horses' coats shining, tails neatly plaited and brasses gleaming in the sunshine!

Two groups of Morris dancers 1916 with bells on their legs and Morris sticks ready. Betty Horne smiles for the camera on the far left.

The Women's Institute in the 1920s outside the town hall. On the left is Mr Bazely who was the caretaker of the grammar school, sexton of the church and, possibly also, caretaker of the town hall. Back row, second from left is Mrs A. Watkins (mother of Miss K.E. Watkins). Mrs Searle, the president, sits in the middle of the front row and on her right is Mrs Bowen Jones, wife of the chemist.

The women's section of Chipping Sodbury British Legion proudly display their trophy in the early 1920s. Among those present on the front row are, from left to right: Miss Emmie Trotman, Miss Nash, Mrs Savery, -?-, -?-, -?-, Miss Leman and Mrs Lediard with Mrs Freeman standing to her left. Back row: Mrs Florence Thompson (8th) Mrs Trotman (13th) and Mrs Warren on the extreme right.

St John the Baptist church choir outing to Southsea in 1928. Back row, left to right: Bruce Newman, John Sorrell, Horace Tily, Bert Crane, Les Williams, Percy Dyer. Front row: ? Williams, Roy Trotman, J. Williams, Harold Stokes. In 1929 choirboys at St John's were paid one penny per attendance at each service and the same for choir practice, with the money being paid quarterly. An attendance register was kept and the money paid by Mrs Bazely, who also kept a strict eye on the choirboys.

The first cinema on this site in Chapel Lane, now Hounds Road, was a wood and canvas construction erected about 1930. Mrs Mott, later to become Mrs Collins, ran the cinema, keeping order by not allowing the children to cheer or stamp their feet. If the film was silent, Mr Morley Bright played incidental music on the piano. The building was eventually blown down by a gale, ending up in the road, and the cinema in this picture was built as a replacement. Mr Watts-Williams owned the cinema in 1945 when all school children up to the age of fourteen were given a free film show to celebrate victory at the end of the war. Mr Watts-Williams was also a milkman and seats for Saturday nights were reserved by means of suitable notes left in empty milk bottles. Later another cinema was built on the corner of Woodmans Road by Mr Harry Dando and called The Glen, after his daughter Glenice.

Chipping Sodbury Pageant was staged in 1935 to celebrate the 400th anniversary of Henry VIII's visit to the town. It was held at Lilliput Court, the site of the former council offices, with over 600 performers and had a grandstand for spectators. Costumes had to be hired and songs were sung in Latin. It was organised by a lady from Colts Green in Old Sodbury and the musical director was Miss Evelyn Bowles. (Miss Bowles died in July 1999 at the age of eighty-eight.)

The Chipping Sodbury Baptist Church Women's Own meeting in 1936, was held as a tea party in the Garden of Rest behind the Baptist chapel. Included in the photograph are: Mrs Dowding, her mother and a friend, Mrs Thompson (former church cleaner) Mrs E. Powell, Mrs Slade, Mrs Ball, Mrs Holder, Mrs Roach, Mrs J. Williams, Mrs B. Lewis, her sister Mrs Moon (wearing dark glasses), Mrs Hillier, Mrs Whiting Snr., Mrs Marjorie Powell, Mrs E. Savory, Miss Mills, Mrs McRied, Mrs Wayman, Miss G. Evans, Miss Ros Evans, Mrs Tom Dando, Miss Iris Tuck, Mrs Glyn Davies and her daughter Lyn, the Woodman children, Miss B. Ball, Mrs Fells, Master Ridley Dowding, Mrs Lumber, the first Mrs Harry Dando, Mrs Hillier, Mrs Lemon, Miss B. Wilkins, Mrs Underwood, Miss L. Trotman, Mrs Roy Trotman.

The 1st Chipping Sodbury Scout Troop at camp on a sunny day at Woodspring Priory near Weston-Super-Mare, 1937. All the equipment for this camp was conveyed by Mr Walter Dunkerley to Woodspring from the scout's hut, situated between the top of Hounds Road and Smarts Green. Here, sitting on a wooden log, beside a paraffin stove and lamp, the boys learned the rudiments of scouting. They also formed the guard of honour at the wedding of their skipper, Harold Turner. From left to right: Bill Newman, Ken Norton, Jack Hawkins, Fred Allen, Ray Pearce, Harold Turner (skipper) Arnold Woodward, Glen Hillier, Marcus Dowding, John Clark.

The very successful tug-of-war team from The Boot, with friends, in the 1940s. They proudly display their trophies won from contests countrywide, including Wembley. From left to right: Ernie Earle, Flo Sullivan, with Roy Colwill in front, Roy Fox, Arthur Dash, Albert Greenaway, Bert Lewis (captain) Walter Jarvis, Gordon Mathews, Tom Hardy, Martin Comber, Fenton Moran, Mr Wiltshire (landlord).

The ladies of the Chipping Sodbury football team were all smiles for this photograph from the 1940s. Back row, left to right: Ethel Jarvis, Phyllis Mayo (*née* Gardener) -?-, Eve Hartill (*née* Wallace) Joan Febry (*née* Norman) -?-. Front row: Betty Willis, Connie Clark (*née* Frost) -?-, Blanche Bird, Brenda Gowan (*née* Parker).

The Mary Livesey School of Dance was in Horse Street, situated where Car Components now trades. The front of the building was an ice-cream parlour and the dance studio was in a wooden building on land at the back. Concerts were performed in the town hall in aid of charity during the 1940s and 1950s.

The Women's Institute in the mid 1950s, in the Quaker Chapel in Brook Street. In the picture can be seen: Iris Ball and her mother, Mrs Bird, Marjorie Warren, Mrs W. Ball, Barbara Lowe, Mrs Crane, Mrs Taylor, Mrs Gerty Williams, May Matthews, Mrs Gladys Lewis, Mrs A. Greenaway, Molly Lewis, Mrs Betty Williams, and Mrs H. Rogers.

The Mop Fair has been held twice a year for centuries. Originally it was a hiring fair with all those looking for work carrying an indication of their job: for example a serving girl would carry a mop. At the beginning of the twentieth century the fair was sited near to the war memorial, but an accident at a shooting booth in 1904 forced it onto the Rag Field (opposite the church) In 1932 it was reinstated in Broad Street where it still thrives to this day.

All the fun of the fair! Dr Haig Sarafian in earnest conversation with members of the Rogers family at a fete in aid of the cottage hospital funds. Seated, left to right: Mrs Ivy Rogers with her daughter June, Mrs Georgina Greenaway and her sister Mrs Annie Rogers. Annie was the daughter of John Coles who was the founder of the local fairground business before the turn of the century. Annie married George Rogers whilst keeping The Bell Inn at Old Sodbury for her father. They met when he called in for a drink, whilst hauling salt by horse and cart from Bristol docks to Stow-on-the-Wold. They carried on the fairground business and were followed on by their sons George, Jack, Percy, Fred and Jimmy. It is now in the control of Mrs Kathleen Rowland, daughter of Percy.

The Over Sixties Club, later the Golden Age Club, in the 1950s, thought to be at the Quaker Chapel in Brook Street. The picture includes: Inspector Ford and his wife, Babs Allen (Mrs W. Evans) Mrs F. Shipp, Mrs H. Sweatman, Mrs A. Greenaway and Mrs Mitchell.

There is evidence that there has been a cricket club in Chipping Sodbury since 1860. A minute book of the Bailiff and Burgesses of the Ancient Borough of Chipping Sodbury shows that renewed permission was given for the club to use the Stubb Riding for cricket in 1861. Cricket will always be associated with the Grace family and in 1860 Dr Alfred Grace came to Chipping Sodbury to take over Dr Brookman's practice in the town. These cricketers were photographed in the 1890s. Back row, left to right: J. Mills, -?-, ? Woodward, Dr Alfred Grace, -?-, W. Turner. Seated at centre: J. Rowe (possibly) and G.H. Eyles. Front row: G. Bates, -?-, Dr T.C. Leman, S.Turner, -?-.

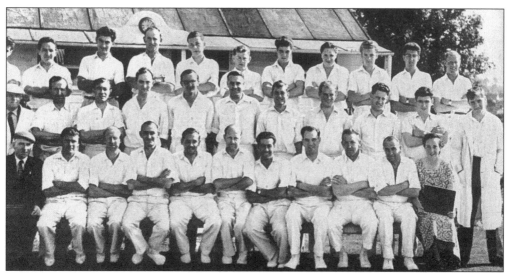

Chipping Sodbury cricketers in 1959. Back row, left to right: T. Leslie, B. Seymour, R. Iles, D. Blanch, Dowding, R, Quinlan, M. Smith, J. Pope, M. Hurford, D. Causon, F. Cowles. Middle row: H.S. King (umpire), R. Wells, E. Purbrick, D. Atkins, V. Harris, J. Stallibrass, G. Wiltshire, J. Griffiths, R. Lewis, D. Febry, M. Vickery. Front row: A. Paul (scorer), P. Freeman, J. Cowles, J. Leslie, P. Guy, J. King, T. Pinnell, N. Buckeridge, W. Backhouse, W. Vickery, Mrs J. Cowles (scorer).

Only enthusiasm for the game, with its revival after the Second World War, could have impelled this group of Chipping Sodbury cricketers to work so hard with no financial reward! The picture shows the erection in 1949 of a pavilion, now replaced, that was acquired from the golf club. Cricket club members manhandled the sections from the Stubb Riding across the cricket ground where it was assembled and renovated. From left to right: Ron Tranter, Jack Sandells, Norman Buckeridge (proud owner of the Austin car), Hugo King, Wally Vickery, John Pettit, Montague Harris, Bridget and Diana Sandells, John King.

Chipping Sodbury football team, 1900. Back row standing, left to right: F. Stovin, J. Penglaze, H. Beasley, J. Goodman, S. Burnell, E, Bees. Second row standing: J. Russell, W.J. Hunt, R.B. Trenfield, A. Hewett, H. Tanner, S. Cowles, R. McCarragher, R.P. Habgood, W. Greenaway, -?-. Front row, seated and kneeling: H.H. Bartlett, W.J. Crane, L.F. Shipway, E.S. Davies (captain), H. Marshall, G.E. Jotcham (hon. sec), P. ?, Front row, reclined: W. Greenaway, H. Lewis. Record: played 28; won 19; lost 8; drawn 1; goals for 80; goals against 45.

Chipping Sodbury Rugby Club, early 1960s. Back row, left to right: Greg Philips, Paul Whittle, Terry Cornock, Mike Woodward, Paul Willis, John Walters, Ian Burbidge, Tony Richings, Mike Thompson, Bill Bennett, Don Wyman, -?-, Bill Tily, Gerry Gibbon, Dick Tily, -?-. Middle row: Reg Philips, Richard Jardine, Terry Williams, Roger Bristow, John Gale, Terry Gwynn, Mike Higgins, Keith Davis, Brian Short. Front row: Dave Jardine, Dave Trotman, Peter Hathaway, Rodney Artingstall, Chris Ladd, Rex Evans, Pete Greenaway, -?-, Peter Mills. This flourishing club celebrates its 50th anniversary in 1999 under the presidency of Paul Whittle after the long reign of Harry Price.

Two

Little Sodbury

Across the ancient common land to the north east of Chipping Sodbury is Little Sodbury, whose population is very small in relation to its neighbours. Yet, centred on the hamlet encompassing St Adeline's church and a further hamlet adjoining the Tyndale Chapel at Little Sodbury End, time seems to have stood still.

The area is a jewel of peace and natural beauty sheltering under the hillside and the Cotswold Way. The wooded slopes reaching out from the ancient manor abound with beech trees, sweet chestnuts and snowdrops in their season. These, together with ancient hedgerows, provide a haven for wildlife.

It was to the manor that the brilliant young scholar William Tyndale came in 1521 as tutor to the children of Sir John Walshe. Here, he began the translation of the New Testament into English from the Greek and also found time to preach in the neighbouring thirteenth-century church. Following conflict with Walshe's brother-in-law Tyndale is reputed to have said 'If God will spare my life I will cause the boy who follows the plough to know more of the Bible than thou dost'. Ironically it was his martyrdom that helped to make this possible.

The ancient church was dismantled in Victorian times and replaced by the present building. Above the woodlands and to the east, man had seemingly toiled long before Christianity. The ancient Iron Age fort, inappropriately known as 'Roman Camps', is a monument to their work.

The 'lowing herds' still browse on the common pastures, sheep still graze on the uplands, corn still shoots on the escarpment: 'the old order changeth not', at least in Little Sodbury.

Church Farm, almost opposite to the school, in 1930 with Mrs Mabel Weaver sitting in the garden. From her three cows she supplied milk to local residents. When she gave up, Tom Bennett of The Gables took over the farm, including the three cows, and one of his workmen moved into the house.

These four pictures show Little Sodbury Manor. There is evidence of a house being on this site since the thirteenth century. In 1485 Richard Forster lived at the manor and his daughter Elizabeth married Sir John Walshe of Alverstone who was a very important man. He and Sir Robert Poyntz were the King's receivers for the Berkeley lands. The manor was part of her marriage settlement and it was at this time that the manor was extensively rebuilt.

William Tyndale was a tutor at the manor for several years from 1521 and it was in 1522 that he started his translation of the New Testament from the Greek into English. In 1535, when Henry VIII and his wife Anne Boleyn were in Thornbury and on their way to Bristol, they were informed that a plague had broken out there. The visit being cancelled they stayed instead at Little Sodbury Manor.

Edward Stephens became High Sheriff of Gloucester 1634 and he inherited Little Sodbury Manor from his father Thomas. He made extensive modifications to the house, panelling rooms and building stone fireplaces carved with coats-of-arms. One fireplace, known as the 'Stephens' fireplace, was removed to Lyegrove House in the nineteenth century. He became a Parliamentarian during the Civil War, supplying horses for the cause. The last member of the Stephens family died in 1728.

In this room, England's greatest treasure was born. The Bible in English.

In the early 1900s it was in a very poor state of repair and during the First World War the owner at that time, Lord Hugh Grosvenor, was killed in action. The manor was purchased by Baron de Tuyll, the Dowager Duchess of Beaufort's son from her first marriage. The Baron then set about carefully restoring the manor and designing the beautiful gardens, although sadly he did not live long enough to enjoy the fruits of his labour. Upon his death the estate was inherited by his cousin, Mark Harford. During the Second World War the manor was used as a rehabilitation centre for servicemen.

A peaceful view of the duck pond, now lost, fronting St Adeline's church and the School House, known as 'The Laurels'. The school was built in 1876, the first head teacher being Miss Prescott, while the vicar at the time was the Revd James Hasluck. In the centre is Baron de Tuyll.

A worker demonstrates an inhumane device known as the man-trap outside the main entrance porch to Little Sodbury Manor in the early 1900s. These were laid mainly in woodland undergrowth to catch unsuspecting poachers.

The Roman Camps outside Little Sodbury. The Romans invaded England in 55 and 54 BC, but it was a further hundred years before they settled to any great extent. At Little Sodbury the Roman army made use of part of what remained of a much bigger British camp already established on the site in Iron Age times (450 BC). The Roman Camp is approximately rectangular in plan and was strongly defended by a series of ditches and banks, accessed via defended causeways. The total defended area was some twelve acres and it has been said that fifteen other camps can be seen from this camp. At the time of the invasion the camp would have housed an agricultural, self-sufficient community with wooden farm buildings and stores. The Romans were to change the primitive local economy by producing food and goods for trading with Roman towns such as Bath and Cirencester.

In the 1880s St Adeline's church, which was situated behind Little Sodbury Manor, was dismantled and the stones taken to help build the new church on its present site near to the village school. Enough stone was left in the old church to show where it had been. When Clive Gunnell made a television programme *Walking the Cotswold Way* he pointed out the fine stone carvings on the arch each side of the front entrance to the present church. He expressed the opinion that they were some of the finest in the country.

The wedding of Mr Percy James and Miss Mabel Grivell at Little Sodbury church, on 19 July 1930. From left to right: Margery Marner, William James, Percy James, Mabel Grivell, Albert Grivell, Joan Deacon, Florrie James, Nan Wigmore. Margery, Mabel and Nan worked together in service, first at The Cottage, Dyrham and later for Colonel Carlysle at Frocester. The Revd Henry Golledge, Rector of Little Sodbury, officiated at the ceremony. Note the carved stone heads on either side of the doorway that appear at first sight to be the heads of other guests!

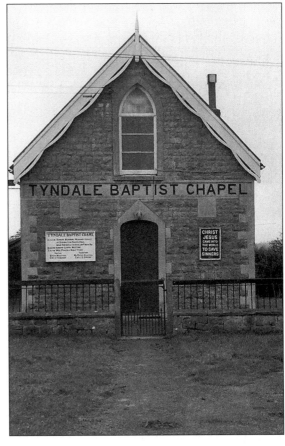

The Tyndale Baptist chapel, is of a typically Victorian design and was built on Sodbury Common at Little Sodbury End in 1890. Before this, Baptists probably worshipped in private houses. The chapel came into existence due to the perseverance of Revd Arthur Parker, the minister at Old Sodbury chapel.

An ancient watering facility shaped in the form of a star, for animals at Cross Hands Farm, adjacent to the Roman camp. The base was cobbled and the water, which was eight feet deep in the middle, came from the guttering on the barns. With the walls extending up into the yards, the pool served the needs of cattle, sheep and shire horses.

The shepherd's hut, carefully restored by Tom Bennett, is almost complete with everything needed for a cold night at lambing time. Missing is the small shepherd's fire which lasted for around two hours, thus enabling the shepherd to know when it was time to make a round of his flock.

Three
Old Sodbury

Rising from the plain to the east of Chipping Sodbury to the high ground surrounding the church, Old Sodbury holds a commanding position over the Severn Vale. There was a long period of Saxon domination before the arrival of William the Conqueror and the subsequent writing of the Domesday Book, in which a mill is mentioned on the site of the present Old Mill. Between 1200 and 1255 a Norman church was established, the mother church to Chipping Sodbury's initial chapel. Some of the original building remains including the tower and part of the nave. In later centuries considerable non-conformist influence brought about the erection of two chapels in Chapel Lane, both now privately owned.

The Dog Inn, Hayes, Pound Cottage, Village Farm and Lower Coombs End Farm likewise have their origins deep in history. Home Farm, now Camers, was probably the situation for the farming activities of a prosperous gentleman named William Davies in the mid seventeenth century. In 1690, having sired eighteen children, he was recognised as a highwayman and, after fleeing to London, was hanged in December of that year.

The Cross Hands Hotel, celebrated for hosting the present Queen on a severe wintry night in 1981, was for many years both the site of a large farm and the site of the Court of Petty Sessions. It prospered particularly at the turn of the century when, by reviving its ancient drinks licence, it served the needs of the hundreds of navvies building the Badminton railway tunnel and railway. The population of Old Sodbury increased dramatically during the six year construction period and changes were made in the village to cope with the works. The school, the Dog Inn and several nearby cottages were extended and a brickworks was established in Chapel Lane. With the River Frome meandering through the nearby meadows, the village still retains it rural surroundings, a communal spirit and a pride in its inheritance.

An English country garden at The Poplars, owned by Mr Stuart Orchard in the 1920s and sometimes called the 'Seed Stores' because people went there to purchase their seeds. It was then sold to Mr and Mrs Rule, she being the producer of the Good Companions dramatic society. Then the house was left empty for some time, only providing shelter for tramps. In the late 1960s it was restored by Mr Margenout and is now the Sodbury House Hotel.

The Cross Hands Hotel, with the Beaufort Hunt in front, was part of the Beaufort Estate in the later years of the nineteenth century and was farmed by Thomas Bennett. At one time the Court of the Petty Sessions were held in what is now the dining room. Thomas Bennet's son, John (Jack) took over on his return from Canada in 1919. At that time many of the outbuildings, including the present conference centre, would have housed shire horses and also hunters on a livery basis.

Arriving at the Cross Hands Hotel in the 1940s adjacent to the original front door with mounting steps for horse riders. Originally a coaching inn, the licence was retained when it became a working farmhouse. This enabled the needs of the hundreds of navvies working on the nearby Badminton railway line and tunnel to be met. The original sign, hanging above the back of the car, carries the inscription *Carius Marius Imperator Concordia Militum* (Carius Marius by consent commander of the army). The inscription came from a Roman coin discovered on the site during restoration work around 1820.

Lower Coombs End Farm, one of the oldest homes in Gloucestershire, as recorded by Linda Hall in *Old Houses of Gloucestershire* for the Royal Commission on Ancient Monuments. The house originated in the fifteenth century with extensions in later years. Restoration in the 1970s revealed an ancient fireplace above which was carved 'G 1654 R'. It is thought that this referred to Gabriel Russell, Comptroller to the Earl of Leicester. A north-facing wall shows the imprint of a hand with 1692 carved across the palm – a mason's mark. The farm was bought in 1919 by Mr John Sherborne and later taken over by his son Stanley who, in 1970, moved to a new home in the grounds.

Backed by the lovely beech trees of Dodington Park these two cottages at Coombs End were photographed in 1910. Mr and Mrs Joe Atherton and Mr and Mrs Pocock lived here until the former landlord of the Dog Inn, Mr Rusty Coward, had them converted into one house in the 1960s.

This cottage stood on the left hand side of Old Sodbury Hill, once known as Dog Hill, before the turning to Cotswold Lane. George White, the roadman, lived there 1900. The cottage was demolished in the early 1970s.

Hill House, which was once occupied by the brewer of the Old Sodbury Brewery. The modern house, called The Maltings, at the top of Old Sodbury Hill, is on the site once occupied by the brewery. Hill House was bought by James Perrett in 1884 and here he built up a thriving business trading under the name of James Mason Perrett and Sons. He owned many inns in the area including the shop and off licence next to Murray Dowding's store in Chipping Sodbury, The Dog and Bell Inn in Old Sodbury and The Cross Keys in Yate.

The Old Mill. From the census of 1891 the mill housed the families of Job Chandler and William Edwards. Mr Chandler was larder butler at Dodington House and his daughter Sarah Anne was assistant at the Old Sodbury National School.

The Old Mill in Fattinghouse Lane, now Mill Lane, 1929 showing Barbara Lloyd at the back door with stabling to the right. Now the home of Mr and Mrs M. Bush, the house today has a very different appearance. The site of the mill is recorded in the Domesday Book and was almost certainly used from mediaeval, if not Saxon, times for corn milling. The corn was drawn probably on sledges, from the Lyegrove area down The Holloway, by Hayes and through the village to the mill.

The Gables, Badminton Road, at Colts Green. This three-storey house was built in 1690 for a Yeoman farmer, with cheeses being stored on the top floor. John Hatherell was a wine importer and seed merchant. He married Elizabeth Ovens and they lived at the house at the end of the nineteenth century. As time went on and their twelve children grew up and left home, the house became too large for them, so Mr Hatherell had a smaller house built next door called Elmgrove. When the railway line from Badminton was in the planning stage it was feared that The Gables would have to be demolished but fortunately the Duke of Beaufort had the line re-routed and the house was saved.

These three cottages in Chapel Lane, known as Elmgrove Cottages, were built in 1875. Next to them is the Baptist chapel of 1835 and the piece of land between the two buildings was known as the 'Barton'. The cottages were used to house the construction managers during the building of the Badminton railway tunnel. Elmgrove Cottages, later known as Chapelgarth, were converted into a single house in the 1940s and the chapel into a private dwelling in the 1960s. The cottages have recently reverted to their original name of Elmgrove.

The Dog Inn was owned by Perretts, as can be seen on the large sign attached to the chimney. The present skittle alley room was built to serve drinks to the navvies during the tunnel construction. To speed up the service the barman simply dipped the mugs into a bath of ale!

On The Green opposite the Dog Inn a fountain was erected to commemorate the Diamond Jubilee of Queen Victoria in 1897. The railings around the fountain were erected by John Jenkins in 1916 at the cost of £16 12s. In 1927 they were removed, which dates the picture to between these times. The fountain now serves as a plant trough. The inn sign has the following inscription, 'This gate hangs well and hinders none, now down/up the hill before you pass, step in and take a cheerful glass.' Blair Cottage is on the left of the Dog Inn.

This idyllic looking thatched cottage once stood on the corner of the Green opposite the Dog Inn. Mr and Mrs Jack Gleed lived there and he looked after the pumping station for the Water Company. When the cottage was pulled down in 1912, they moved to a new brick-built Water Company house just around the corner on the Badminton Road. On the left, seen here in about 1910, is Mrs Gleed, holding Cyril in her arms (Cyril worked for Bristol Water and continued to live in the family home in later years). Next to Mrs Gleed is Lily with Bob and Bill holding hands. Behind them is Nellie (mother of Mrs Mabel Clift), Mr Gleed and Walter.

Cotswold Lane leading to the church. On the right hand side is the pumping station that was erected in 1897 by the West Gloucestershire Water Company. After this the old wells and pumps gradually fell into disuse.

Cotswold Lane in the early 1920s. Norton Cottage is on the left, the next thatched cottage is School Cottage, and further up the hill is Yew Tree Cottage. On the right is Myrtle House, now named Myrtle Cottage. The children standing in the road could well be the Febry family, since Myrtle House was their home. School Cottage was built 1840 and was once owned by F.W.W. Winchcombe Hartley from Lyegrove; in fact he owned twenty-eight out of the ninety one cottages in Old Sodbury at one time. The church in the background was covered in ivy until the First World War, which helps date this picture.

Time stands still at Hayes, adjacent to the church. Built in about 1600 by Walter Walshe, Lord of the Manor, it passed into the ownership of Thomas Stephens around 1607/8, although he remained at Little Sodbury Manor. He was Attorney General to the Royal Princes, Henry and Charles, later Charles I. The house was sold to the Collwell family in 1732, Susannah Collwell married the Revd William Dixon in 1710 and their descendants retained ownership of it until 1907. It was then purchased by Mr A.W. Brooks and has remained in the family possession until the present time.

The turning into Church Lane from Old Sodbury Hill 1910. The children are standing by a motorbike and side-car belonging to Nurse Self who used it to travel around fulfilling her duties as district nurse and mid-wife. The distant cottage on the right was the Matthews' family bakery. The building on the left was used by them as a store but it later became an ex-servicemen's club.

A spring day at the turn of the century looking down from Southcroft into Church Lane, with the school on the right. Opposite is a building comprising two dwelling houses, known as Heclan House and the Old School House, on either side of an archway at the front. The property was sold in 1928 on the death of Mr W.B. Brooks and was catalogued as having 'a front room, kitchen, back porch, outside wash-house and other offices, large landing used as a bedroom and two other bedrooms'.

The Vicarage in Church Lane, at the turn of the century, which is now a guest house called Dornden. The sweep of the garden stays very much the same with a wonderful massed display of snowdrops in springtime. Past incumbents have been Robert S. Nash 1856-1905 and Daniel Wrigley 1905-1916.

St John's church stands proudly on the hill leading up from Common Mead Lane. Belonging to the See of Worcester after the Norman Conquest, this village church was built between 1215 and 1225. Of the original building only the tower, part of the nave, the south door and the two windows in the north and south aisles remain within the present church. It was in the original sturdy tower that the clock was installed much later to celebrate Queen Victoria's Jubilee. To the left of the tower is a path leading to a small iron gate beyond which can be seen magnificent views of the surrounding countryside.

These two photographs provide an opportunity for an interesting comparison to be made over a period of many years. Note the earlier picture does not have the clock and the slow growing Yew tree can barely be seen.

The interior of the church, shown here in the early 1900s, shows clearly the influence of the Normans. The double row of pillars in the nave, the inner door of the south porch with its crown of thorn decorations and the small window at the west end were all built in this period. The chancel, which had been extended by some eight to nine feet, is entered under a pointed arch in the Early English style. In the north transept are effigies of two knights, one from the thirteenth century lying cross-legged and covered by his shield all carved in stone and the other of the fourteenth century carved in wood. The identity of both knights and what they represent is unknown. The font, just visible to the right of the picture, is from the fifteenth century.

The lychgate was built as a war memorial to honour the dead of the First World War. The names of the fallen have been carved on the inside beams. On wedding days children of the village tie the gates together and will not untie them until the bridegroom throws them a few coins.

As the midnight hour approaches the church can be seen floodlit in 1937 for the Coronation of George VI and Queen Elizabeth, now the Queen Mother.

The Bishop of Gloucester outside the church between its two churchwardens, on the left Mr Seymour Williams and on the right Mr Brooks. To the right is the vicar, the Revd Henry Burgess, who served the church from 1918-55 and who was a very popular and respected cleric.

The Tyndale chapel manse was built in Chapel Lane, once known as Dog Lane, in 1892. The minister's living was the chapel, a few doors away to the left. Outside in the front garden are seated the Revd Arthur Parker and his family. Leaning over the fence is Bob Parker who was sadly killed during the First World War on 19 April 1918. Mrs Parker is to the left of the front door and beside her is Dorothy who later married Stanley Perrett and is the mother of Mr David Perrett, the veterinary surgeon. Whilst the house was being built the family stayed in the middle cottage of Chapelgarth, then known as Elmgrove Cottages. On the right are some old cottages, now pulled down to make way for modern housing.

The Revd Arthur Parker by the front gate of the middle cottage of Elmgrove Cottages. The front door was blocked up in the 1940s when the cottages were converted into a single house by Michael Searle, the veterinary surgeon, and renamed Chapelgarth.

Old Sodbury. Baptist Sunday School

The Baptist chapel, in Chapel Lane, opened a Sunday school in the mid 1920s and about thirty-five children were enrolled. The two Miss Haywards were the mainstays of the school. The resident minister living in the manse, Chapel Lane, was also in charge of a circuit of small chapels in the area.

The fire cart which was kept in a shed behind the village hall 1900. Captain Gee was in charge of fire operations in the village and he lived at Church Farm, which is on the green facing Chapel Lane.

The workmen on the line celebrating the completion of the two mile long railway tunnel from Badminton to Old Sodbury. Fifth from the left is James Henry Williams. The tunnel was built between 1898 and 1903 by S. Pearson and Son as part of the 33-mile long improvement to the GWR line between Wootton Bassett and Patchway It was dug outwards from seven access shafts each 12ft in diameter, the deepest being 279ft. The tunnel is brick-lined using bricks made in the Old Sodbury brickworks, off Chapel Lane, with clay excavated from the workings. Six of the shafts were retained as ventilation shafts and topped with 35ft high towers and surrounded by landscaped material excavated from the tunnel. The tunnel cost approximately £252,000 to build and it has been estimated that some 320,000 cubic yards of material were excavated. At the height of the works some 600 itinerant workers were billeted in the area, either in private homes or in specially set up camps, including a shanty town on Kingrove Common.

The tunnel, a few years later, showing how close it is to Old Sodbury. One can imagine what effect the influx of so many workers into the area would have had on the village.

A down train negotiating floods leaving the Badminton railway tunnel in 1909. Water has always been a problem in the tunnel from the time that construction started. A large culvert was laid below the tunnel invert to deal with water flows in excess of half a million gallons a day coming into the tunnel from the surrounding ground.

Bringing the coal home from Badminton Station 1930/31. On the left is Bert Thatcher from Swindon and on the right is Charlie Walker. They have stopped by Lyegrove Cottages.

A Gloucestershire County Council Foden steam wagon in the early 1930s. From left to right: Sam Deacon, 'Mustard' Stinchcombe, Thomas Wigmore Snr, Leslie Shipp.

A tractor with trailer stops to be photographed in Kingrove Common by the railway line in 1919. The trailer seems to come from Bedminster and the four people are still in uniform and were perhaps stationed locally.

The Badminton railway tunnel was one of the more strategic points on the railway network which it was feared would become an obvious target for German sabotage during the First World War. In 1914 guards were deployed at important points including the main tunnel and the tops of the ventilation shafts. At the outbreak of war the guards were railway staff with very primitive weapons but the army soon took over the duties. Three soldiers from the Loyal North Lancs. Regiment pose for the photograph (right) and Private Babbage is seen on duty (below) at Christmas!

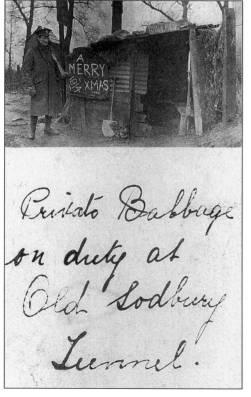

Private Babbage on duty at Old Sodbury Tunnel.

On the home front during the First World War the women did the haymaking in the fields. They took over whilst their men-folk were away fighting abroad. Everyone did their bit for the war effort, such as collecting hedgerow fruits – even the children were given time off school to collect blackberries.

Providence Place, to the left on the Badminton Road, comprising the Old Post Office on the left end and Providence House on the right. Above the post office door can be seen three stone figures, all tailors sitting cross-legged. The stone mason was Samson Lockstone who owned the cottages 1840. He was a fine craftsman having worked in stone on the Royal Pavilion, Brighton and carving the Griffin on the top of Chippenham Lodge, the entrance to Dodington House. In the 1930s Mary Uzzell owned the post office and in July 1930 she sold the three tailors to Mr A.C. Brooks at Hayes for £3 on condition that they stayed above the door during her lifetime. She died in 1937 and the little figures were taken to their new owner. Beyond are Mrs Radford's cottage, Winnie Webb's cottage, where sweets were sold from a shed at the side, and then Ada Deane's cottage. Miss Deane had once worked at St James' Palace in London.

'Oh dear, what can the matter be?' This three-seater was found at Parks Farm and no doubt similar ones were installed at the cottages above. Usually housed at the bottom of the garden amidst dense evergreens, the privy could be a frightening place for the user of the smallest seat!

J Jenkins' shoeing forge, before it became a garage, in the early 1900s. The cottages can still be found behind the modern forecourt of the petrol station.

Badminton Road in the late 1930s, with the three stone figures no longer above the post office door. Beyond is the Water Works house and further on, by the turning to Cotswold Lane, is the garage where there was once the blacksmith's forge. Nearest to the camera is Mrs Radford's cottage.

The 'General and Fancy Drapers' shop, on the green 1910-20. Mr and Mrs Biagioli are the present owners but it is no longer a shop. At one time there were nine shops in the village.

An elegant study of the Fry sisters in the 1890s, from the left Lena, Ada and Lizzie. Lena became Tom Wigmore's mother.

Mr and Mrs John Hatherell sitting in the front garden at Elmgrove at the turn of the century. Sitting between them on the garden seat is, once again, Murray Dowding's famous terrier Puck. John Hatherell died in 1902 at the age of sixty eight and his wife Elizabeth died in 1919 aged seventy-five.

Outside Matthews' bakery in Church Lane, 1902, is Alice Haughton with her bicycle. Alice became the church organist and was the sister of Arthur Matthews, a well known personality.

Mrs Ann Walker, in 1911, who was grandmother to nearly one hundred family descendants. One of her sons, Isaac and his wife Marie, can be seen in their cottage garden opposite to the entrance of Lyegrove House, on the way to Badminton. Marie did the washing for the Westmorlands, the owners of Lyegrove, and Isaac was the head shepherd. They were the parents of Charles Walker.

In her Sunday best in 1907 and looking intently at the camera is May Redman, later to become Mrs Joe Atherton. A keen member of the Women's Institute, she was secretary for many years and also its president. Mr Atherton farmed with Mr Bill Pullin at Home Farm, Dodington.

Frank and Emily Bennett in their garden at New Road, now Badminton Road. A member of the church choir at Old Sodbury for many years, Frank spent most of his working life at Plough Farm. At the same time Emily worked very hard in domestic service at the adjacent Cross Hands Farm.

Ernest Bennett, son of Frank and Emily Bennett, standing complete with walking stick, watch chain and cigarette at the stile leading into The Close, some time before 1914, where there is now a kissing gate. During the First World War he worked in the mines at Bedwas, in South Wales, and remained in that area for the rest of his life.

A First World War family group, in 1915. Frank Trotman, seen here with photographer Murray Dowding's dog taking a front seat, was a printer by trade. He volunteered for the Somerset Light Infantry in 1914 and was wounded on the Somme in 1916. Upon recovery he returned to the front only to suffer severe shell shock in 1917. He was in hospital in Felixstowe and ultimately returned in 1918 to Chipping Sodbury and into the care of Dr Alfred Grace. He spent the rest of his life working in the Sodbury area. With him in the photograph, taken in the garden of their home in the Badminton Road, are from left to right: Catherine, Margaret, with baby Maurice, and Phyllis.

Joe Atherton, 6 August 1918. Joe volunteered for service as soon as the First World War broke out, adding several years to his age to make himself eligible to join. He was posted to France with the Bristol Own Regiment and took ammunition to the front line on horseback. On one occasion when an explosion blasted him from his horse a sergeant bawled, 'Who told that man to dismount?'

Mr and Mrs Brooks on the right playing croquet on the lawn at Hayes in the 1920s.

Thomas George Wigmore and his wife Lena with their children in the 1920s. Charles is seated to the left and Thomas is standing on the right. Standing at the back from the left are Nan, Eva and Joyce.

Mr Arthur Batten and his wife Ruby on their wedding day, 6 June 1923. Mr Batten farmed for many years at Frome Farm on the Badminton Road.

A wedding on 3 April 1925. Front row, left to right: Gladys Wintle, May Wintle, Fred Wintle (groom), Eva Wintle (nee Wigmore, the bride) Joyce and Nan Wigmore. Back row: George and Emily Wintle (groom's parents) William Wintle (best man) Lena and Thomas George Wigmore (bride's parents). The vicar of Old Sodbury at the time was the Revd Charles H. Gough.

Two smart young ladies in Brownie uniforms and a young gentleman in the uniform of the Cubs, 1930, in the garden of what is now West View, Badminton Road. From the left to right: Inez Hall, Phyllis Hood, Lyndon Hall. Sadly, Inez died of meningitis at the age of sixteen.

Mabel and Percy James, who farmed at Plough Farm next to the Cross Hands Hotel, seen on their motorbikes in the 1930s. A fine horseman, Percy hunted with the Beaufort Hunt and Mabel was a parish councillor, church warden and president of Old Sodbury Women's Institute for many years.

A large family group at the wedding of Catherine Trotman and Alfred Farmery in 1933, photographed in the garden of Hail Close, the home of Mr Will Sprackman. Standing at the back, left to right: Winifred, Florence, Roy and Emily Trotman, Charles Wigmore, Alfred and Catherine, Maurice Trotman, Louise Davis, Sidney and Ruth Box, Phyllis Trotman. Seated: Winifred Read, with her son Mervyn, Frank and Margaret Trotman, Rachael and John Box. Sitting on the lawn: Ruby, Norman and Jack Trotman.

Christmas Day 1934 at Hill View in Church Lane. Mr Sydney Russell (born 1870) and Mrs Sabina Russell (born 1864) stand in their decorative porch on this festive day. Mr Russell was clerk and sexton of Old Sodbury church from 1910 to 1937. His brother Elijah was a blacksmith at Tormarton.

Mr and Mrs Albert Febry with their family of six boys and six girls at Myrtle House in Cotswold Lane in the 1930s. Back row, left to right: Clara, Fred, Bessie, Frank, Jo, Bert, Queen. Middle row: Mabel, Mr and Mrs Febry, Dick, Bill. Front row: Jean, Peggy.

Bert Febry bought this, his first lorry, with money saved during the Second World War when he was a POW in Germany. All was well until Nationalisation when, like other hauliers, he was forced to give up. After de-nationalisation he set up business again, trading as F. and A.G. Febry.

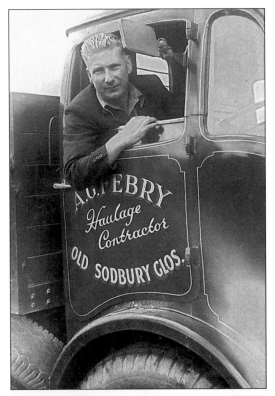

A presentation to Sally, Duchess of Westminster, by little Miss Kendal at a garden party at Old Sodbury House, home of Mr and Mrs Wedmore in the mid-1950s. From the left is the Revd Sydney Thomas, vicar of Old Sodbury from 1955-61, Mabel James, church warden, Sally, Duchess of Westminster, Mrs Wedmore and Edward Seymour Williams. The latter was the auctioneer and estate agent whose business was at Hartley House (now Darlows) in Chipping Sodbury. He was also chairman of Sodbury Parish Council for many years.

Resting her arm on the back of her chair is Miss Holborow outside the front porch of her school at Springrove 1902. Her pupils of six boys and ten girls face the camera together with the assistant in the back row. Dorothy Parker is in the white dress in the middle of the second row and her brother Rob is standing next to the batsman who is wearing a boater.

When the Badminton railway tunnel was under construction (1897-1903) there was a sudden rise in the population as workers arrived with their families. To accommodate the children at the village school, a new hut was added which can be seen to the left of the photograph. After the tunnel was completed in 1903 the extension was removed and taken to Hayes, next to the church, where it was used for many years as a storage shed.

The school in 1921. As far as one of the pupils, Tom Wigmore (then aged nine), can recall, the pupils are, front row, left to right: -?-, -?-, Charlie Wigmore, Cyril Pullen, -?-, -?-, Florence Webb, rest unknown. Second row: -?-, Kathleen Hoare, -?-, Rosie Langdon, -?-, -?-, Mary Freeman, rest unknown. Centre group: Mrs Iles, Frank Wotton, Mr Frank Iles. Third row: -?-, Maurice Trotman, -?-, Tom Wigmore, Cyril Gleed, Rowland Causon, Vivian Wicks, -?-, -?-, -?- , Alfred Hillier. Back row: Florence Field, Maisie Langdon, Phyllis Trotman, ? Self, -?-, -?-, Marie Lloyd, -?-, Nan Wigmore, Kitty Woodman, Bessie Febry.

The school 1928/29. Back row, left to right: Miss Winnie Buoy, -?-, Sonny Gardener, Harry Berry, Philip Murden, Doreen Flooks, Doris Febry, Phyllis Hood, -?-, Betty Flooks, -?-, Ruby Scrivens, Muriel Dolman, Miss Turner with her hands on Peggy White's shoulders. Middle row: Jim Flooks, Stan Sherborne, Jack Harper, -?-, Leslie Hares, Arthur Berry, Louis Febry, ? Hulbert, Raymond Millhouse, Queen Febry, Mabel Harper, Joan Hulbert, Nancy Lewis, Peggy Smith, -?-. Front row: Joan White, -?-, -?-, Anne Sherborne, Desmond Smith, Jean Febry, Peggy Febry, -?-, Barbara Harper, Les Wickes, ? Perks, -?-, -?-.

Visitors to the school from a school in Bournmouth in the 1940s, with some very smart young ladies showing off the latest fashion in handbags. Old Sodbury pupils, back row, left to right: Mervyn Rushant, John Dyer, Monica Hillier, Maureen Hillier, Mr Gill (a teacher at the Old Sodbury School), Suzanne James, Elizabeth Iles, -?-, a visiting teacher wearing a trilby hat. In front of him is Enid Witt and beside him is Gracie Fields. Rita Deane is second from the end sitting on the wall. Mr Stokes, also an Old Sodbury school teacher, is on the far left of the front row. Everybody, including the visitors, appear to be enjoying themselves.

Martin Walker concentrating hard on his lessons in the school in the early 1950s. Mrs V. Slocombe was the head teacher and Mrs Turner her assistant.

A 'nutting party' to the Lower Woods in the autumn 1900 to gather hazelnuts. The family and friends of Mrs Mary Perrett break for a picnic. Mrs Perrett is the lady wearing black. The gentlemen are well prepared with stout sticks to hook down the branches.

The ford by The Old Mill in Fattinghouse Lane, now Mill Lane, with the pedestrian footbridge, in about 1927. Stepping across the stones are Irene Tudor, on the left, and Marie Lloyd, who both lived at the mill. Although the stream has now been culverted and the footbridge is long gone, some things don't change as the children still prefer to wade through the stream rather than use the bridge.

'I promise to do my duty'. The Brownie Pack outside their meeting hut in the vicarage garden 1928/29. Sitting cross-legged in the front row, on either side of the Brownie toadstool and owl are: Jean Febry, Peggy Febry, Barbara Harper, Joan White. The three girls in the middle row are: -?-, Cicily Hunt, Ruby Trotman. Back row: -?-, Peggy White, Pam Brinton (Tawny Owl) Betty Burgess (Brown Owl and daughter of the Revd Burgess) Phyllis Hood, Clare and Pam Norton.

A shooting party from Old Sodbury on Salisbury Plain, 1936. Charles Wigmore is third from the right. He was chauffeur and gardener to Mr A.C. Brooks at Hayes, who is fifth from the right.

The Women's Institute in the 1930s. Back row, left to right: Mrs Couzens (mother of Percy Couzens) Mrs Bessie Bristow, Mrs Kath Sawyer, Mrs Ada Iles, Mrs Jessie Hood, Mrs Beatrice Williams. Front row: Mrs Clara Seymour, Mrs Alice Thomas, Mrs Nora Earle, Mrs Elizabeth Jenkins, Mrs Berry (Mrs Iles' mother) Mrs Alice Febry, Mrs Neale.

Concert at the Good Companions in the early 1940s. This was a flourishing concert party of both young and old who put on shows to raise money for charity. Back row, left to right: Gracie Fields, Elizabeth Iles, Bessie Febry, Diana Febry, Jill Atherton, Freda Short, Kath Sawyer, Peggy Febry, Ada Iles, Clara Seymour. Middle row: Rita Deane, Brian Seymour, Roger Bristow, Enid Witt, Rose Hicks, Anne Wallhead, Ethel Febry, Graham Hinton, Derek Febry. Front row: Viva Witt, Pat Rawlings, June Febry, Sylvia Shipp, Patricia Febry, Enid Shipp.

Old Sodbury Youth Club at the village hall in the 1950s. Amongst the party-goers are: Frank Hillier, Bernard Townsend, Norman Townsend, Patrick Beazer, Brian Seymour, Derek Febry, Brian Gardener, Roger Bristow, Roland Febry, Clive Young, Brian Dash, Gordon Williams, Chris Pople. Front row: Maureen Hillier, Rikka Smith, Monica Hillier, Elizabeth Wintle and Anne Bond.

Bowling for a pig? Tony Matthews shows his paces on the football field at Old Sodbury during the village fête in the 1950s. Standing, left to right: -?-, Charlie Walker, Frank Stinchcombe, Frank Febry, Winnie Stinchcombe, Dudley Matthews, Frank Harper, Margaret Harper. Sitting: Freda Febry, Mabel Clift with June Febry the little girl in front and Terry Matthews on the right.

The Women's Institute had a flourishing drama group during the 1960s. The mini-pantomime *Cinderella* was performed to packed houses in the village hall in 1966. In the front row from the left are Helen Adams, June Roach, Veronica Wintle and Jeannette Bray who were villagers. In the middle row on the left is Sheila Bullock, one of the Ugly Sisters, with Cherry Bush as the other one. Mary Batten was the town crier and Mabel James the fairy Tinkerbell. The other two fairies were Pat Adams and Corrie Ford.

A team of ladies from Old Sodbury who played football against a team of wounded soldiers during the Second World War. The soldiers were recuperating at Little Sodbury Manor, then used as a military hospital, where staff included Miss Grace Sprackman, who still lives in the village. Back row, left to right: Peggy Febry, Bessie Febry, Irene Tudor, Ciss Trace, Winnie Norman. Front row: Jean Febry, Gwen Walker, Jean Burcombe, Clara Febry, Phyllis Gardener.

Old Sodbury football team in 1920/21, outside the Dog Inn. Back row, left to right: S. Wotton, -?-, W. Taylor, Hicks, N. Chandler, G. Hood, -?-, W. Bennett. Front row: H. Chandler, F. Wintle, -?-, -?-, A. Gleed, -?-, -?-, J. Hood.

Old Sodbury football team in 1924/25, on the pitch opposite the post office. Standing, left to right: G. Wintle (trainer), G. Hood, W. Taylor, N. Chandler, J. Hicks, A. Curtis, J. Walker, W. Gleed. Sitting: F. Hood, Frank Marklove, H. White, W. Wotton, F. Wintle, B. Hood, T. Shellard.

Old Sodbury football team, 1934/35. Back row, left to right: Albert Febry, Frank Boucher, Cyril Pullin, Pip Godwin, Glen Hillier, Charlie Walker, Don Richings, Eli Berry, Revd Henry Burgess. Front row: Frank Walker, Harry Berry, Frank Evans, Bert Seymour, Freddie Wintle, Jack Trotman, George Walker.

Old Sodbury football team, 1969/70. Back row, left to right: K. Lucas, D. Orchard, B. Hawkins, M. Smith, P. Davis, D. Knowle, ? Pick. Front row: B. Gardner, D. Fisher, L. Walker, B. Player, M. Walker.

Old Sodbury cricket team at Dodington Park in the 1950s. Back row standing, left to right: Arthur Matthews, Larry Spencer, Charlie Wigmore, Tom Bennett, Cyril Pullin, Les Heaven, John Hinder, George walker. Middle row: Arthur Gleed, Ewart Richings, -?-, Percy Pick. Front row: Albert Greenaway.

Finally, while a younger generation of men were away fighting in Flanders and France, women joined an older group of men in this traditional hay-making scene from 1916. This photograph pays tribute to the skill and artistry of Murray Dowding in depicting a welcome break for the horses and hay-makers in Old Sodbury Fields.